AMERICAN

SMOOTH

OTHER BOOKS BY RITA DOVE

The Yellow House on the Corner (poems, 1980)

Museum (poems, 1983)

Fifth Sunday (short stories, 1985)

Thomas and Beulah (poems, 1986)

Grace Notes (poems, 1989)

Through the Ivory Gate (novel, 1992)

Selected Poems (1993)

The Darker Face of the Earth (verse drama, 1994)

Mother Love (poems, 1995)

The Poet's World (essays, 1995)

On the Bus with Rosa Parks (poems, 1999)

AMERICAN SMOOTH

poems

RITA DOVE

W. W. Norton & Company
New York London

For information about permission to reproduce selections from this book, write to
Permissions, W. W. Norton & Company, Inc., 500 Fifth Avenue, New York, NY 10110

Manufacturing by Courier Westford
Production manager: Julia Druskin

Library of Congress Cataloging-in-Publication Data
Dove, Rita.
American smooth : poems / Rita Dove.— 1st ed.
p. cm.
Includes bibliographical references.
ISBN 0-393-05987-1 (hardcover)
1. National characteristics, American—Poetry. 2. African Americans—Poetry. I. Title.
PS3554.O884A77 2004
811'.54—dc22

2004011793

W. W. Norton & Company, Inc., 500 Fifth Avenue, New York, N.Y. 10110
www.wwnorton.com

W. W. Norton & Company Ltd., Castle House, 75/76 Wells Street, London W1T 3QT

1 2 3 4 5 6 7 8 9 0

for Fred & Aviva

American (ə-mĕr′ĭ-kən) *adj.* **1.** Of or relating to the United States of America or its people, language, or culture.

smooth (smooth) *adj.* **1.** Having a surface free from irregularities, roughness, or projections: even. . . . **2.** Having a fine texture: *a smooth fabric.* . . . **4.** Having an even consistency: *a smooth pudding.* **5.** Having an even or gentle motion or movement: *a smooth ride.* **6.** Having no obstructions or difficulties: *a smooth operation.* **7.** Serene: *a smooth temperament.* **8.** Bland: *a smooth wine.* **9.** Ingratiatingly polite and agreeable. See Synonyms at suave. **10.** Having no grossness or coarseness in dress or manner.

American Smooth *n.* A form of ballroom dancing derived from the traditional Standard dances (e.g., Waltz, Fox Trot, Tango), in which the partners are free to release each other from the closed embrace and dance without any physical contact, thus permitting improvisation and individual expression.

CONTENTS

FOX TROT FRIDAYS 13

All Souls' 15

"I have been a stranger in a strange land" 17

Fox Trot Fridays 19

Ta Ta Cha Cha 20

Quick 22

Brown 23

Fox 25

Heart to Heart 26

Cozy Apologia 28

Soprano 30

Two for the Montrose Drive-In 32

Meditation at Fifty Yards, Moving Target 36

American Smooth 39

NOT WELCOME HERE 41

The Castle Walk 43

The Passage 46

Noble Sissle's Horn 57

Alfonzo Prepares to Go Over the Top 59

La Chapelle. 92nd Division. Ted. 60

Variation on Reclamation 62

The Return of Lieutenant James Reese Europe 65

Ripont 67

TWELVE CHAIRS 71

BLUES IN HALF-TONES, 3/4 TIME 87

Chocolate 89

Bolero 90

Hattie McDaniel Arrives at the Coconut Grove 92

Samba Summer 95

Blues in Half-Tones, 3/4 Time 97

Describe Yourself in Three Words or Less 99

The Seven Veils of Salomé 100

From Your Valentine 104

Rhumba 107

The Sisters: Swansong. 112

EVENING PRIMROSE 115

Evening Primrose 117

Reverie in Open Air 118

Sic Itur Ad Astra 119

Count to Ten and We'll Be There 121

Eliza, Age 10, Harlem 122

Lullaby 123

Driving Through 125

Desert Backyard 127

Desk Dreams 128

Now 132

Against Flight 134

Looking Up from the Page, I Am Reminded
   of This Mortal Coil 136

Notes 139
Acknowledgments 141
Biographical Note 143

FOX TROT FRIDAYS

Do you think you could possibly behave
a little less like yourself?

All Souls'

Starting up behind them,
all the voices of those they had named:
mink, gander, and marmoset,
crow and cockatiel.
Even the duck-billed platypus,
of late so quiet in its bed,
sent out a feeble cry signifying
grief and confusion, et cetera.

Of course the world had changed
for good. As it would from now on
every day, with every twitch and blink.
Now that change was de rigueur,
man would discover desire, then yearn
for what he would learn to call
distraction. This was the true loss.
And yet in that first

unchanging instant,
the two souls
standing outside the gates
(no more than a break in the hedge;
how had they missed it?) were not
thinking. Already the din was fading.
Before them, a silence
larger than all their ignorance

yawned, and this they walked into
until it was all they knew. In time
they hunkered down to business,
filling the world with sighs—
these anonymous, pompous creatures,
heads tilted as if straining
to make out the words to a song
played long ago, in a foreign land.

"I have been a stranger in a strange land"

Life's spell is so exquisite, everything
conspires to break it.
                              —EMILY DICKINSON

It wasn't bliss. What was bliss
but the ordinary life? She'd spend hours
in patter, moving through whole days
touching, sniffing, tasting . . . exquisite
housekeeping in a charmed world.
And yet there was always

more of the same, all that happiness,
the aimless Being There.
So she wandered for a while, bush to arbor,
lingered to look through a pond's restive mirror.
He was off cataloging the universe, probably,
pretending he could organize
what was clearly someone else's chaos.

That's when she found the tree,
the dark, crabbed branches
bearing up such speechless bounty,
she knew without being told
this was forbidden. It wasn't
a question of ownership—
who could lay claim to
such maddening perfection?

And there was no voice in her head,
no whispered intelligence lurking
in the leaves—just an ache that grew
until she knew she'd already lost everything
except desire, the red heft of it
warming her outstretched palm.

Fox Trot Fridays

Thank the stars there's a day
each week to tuck in

the grief, lift your pearls, and
stride brush stride

quick-quick with a
heel-ball-toe. Smooth

as Nat King Cole's
slow satin smile,

easy as taking
one day at a time:

one man and
one woman,

rib to rib,
with no heartbreak in sight—

just the sweep of Paradise
and the space of a song

to count all the wonders in it.

Ta Ta Cha Cha

One, two—no, five doves
scatter before a wingtip's
distracted tread.
Lost, lost, they coo, and
they're probably right:
It's Venice, I'm American,
besandaled and backpacked,
sunk in a bowl of sky
trimmed with marbled statuary
(slate, snow, ash)—
a dazed array, dipped
in the moon's cold palette.

Who, you? No. But here,
lost from a wing, drifts
one pale, italicized
answer. I pick it up
as the bold shoe
continues conversation
(*one two*) with its mate,
and the nearest scavenger
skips three times
to the side, bobs to pluck
his crackerjack prize, a child's
dropped gelato cone.

Tip, tap: early warning code
for afternoon rain. Gray
vagabond, buffoon messenger
for grounded lovers—where to?
Teach me this dance
you make, snatching a sweet
from the path of a man
who, because he knows
where he's headed, walks
without seeing, face hidden
by a dirty wingspan
of the daily news.

Quick

Look, a baby one! Wink of fuzz
in the headlights, and gray at that.

Now he peers from the culvert,
all bobble and twitch, vacant eyes:

he's been through this bait and switch
all night. *Where's mother?*

On the hill, there—crested
in moonshine the fabled silhouette,

sleek curve plumpening into a tail
waving its flamboyant

afterthought, she disappears:
red swish

or gray, too quick to tell.
O to be gone

like that, no grief nor thought
of love—pure purpose

poured into flight.

Brown

Why you look good in every color!
the dress lady gurgled, just before
I stepped onto the parquet
for a waltz. I demurred;
we were in a country club,
after all, and she—fresh
from Fort Lauderdale (do people
actually live there?) with five
duffle bags' worth of ball gowns,
enough tulle and fringe and pearls
to float a small cotillion—
was only trying to earn a living.
For once I was not the only
black person in the room
(two others, both male).
I thought of Sambo; I thought
a few other things, too,
unmentionable here. Don't
get me wrong: I've always loved
my skin, the way it glows against
citron and fuchsia, the difficult hues,
but the difference I cause
whenever I walk into a polite space

is why I prefer grand entrances—
especially with a Waltz,
that European constipated
swoon.

The dress in question was red.

Fox

She knew what
she was and so
was capable
of anything
anyone
could imagine.
She loved what
she was, there
for the taking,
imagine.

She imagined
nothing.
She loved
nothing more
than what she had,
which was enough
for her,
which was more
than any man
could handle.

Heart to Heart

It's neither red
nor sweet.
It doesn't melt
or turn over,
break or harden,
so it can't feel
pain,
yearning,
regret.

It doesn't have
a tip to spin on,
it isn't even
shapely—
just a thick clutch
of muscle,
lopsided,
mute. Still,
I feel it inside
its cage sounding
a dull tattoo:
I want, I want—

but I can't open it:
there's no key.
I can't wear it
on my sleeve,
or tell you from
the bottom of it
how I feel. Here,
it's all yours, now—
but you'll have
to take me,
too.

Cozy Apologia
—for Fred

I could pick anything and think of you—
This lamp, the wind-still rain, the glossy blue
My pen exudes, drying matte, upon the page.
I could choose any hero, any cause or age
And, sure as shooting arrows to the heart,
Astride a dappled mare, legs braced as far apart
As standing in silver stirrups will allow—
There you'll be, with furrowed brow
And chain mail glinting, to set me free:
One eye smiling, the other firm upon the enemy.

This post-post-modern age is all business: compact disks
And faxes, a do-it-now-and-take-no-risks
Event. Today a hurricane is nudging up the coast,
Oddly male: Big Bad Floyd, who brings a host
Of daydreams: awkward reminiscences
Of teenage crushes on worthless boys
Whose only talent was to kiss you senseless.
They all had sissy names—Marcel, Percy, Dewey;
Were thin as licorice and as chewy,
Sweet with a dark and hollow center. Floyd's

Cussing up a storm. You're bunkered in your
Aerie, I'm perched in mine
(Twin desks, computers, hardwood floors):
We're content, but fall short of the Divine.
Still, it's embarrassing, this happiness—
Who's satisfied simply with what's good for us,
When has the ordinary ever been news?
And yet, because nothing else will do
To keep me from melancholy (call it blues),
I fill this stolen time with you.

Soprano

When you hit
the center

of a note, spin
through and off

the bell lip
into heaven,

the soul dies
for an instant—

but you don't need
its thin

resistance
nor the room

(piano shawl,
mirror, hyacinth)

dissolving
as one note

pours into
the next, pebbles

clean as moonspill
seeding a path . . .

and which is it,
body or mind,

which rises, which
gives up at last

and goes home?

Two for the Montrose Drive-In

TUPPERWARE

Three days before it was pick-up-and-scrub,
the tops of doorjambs wiped clean
for white gloves come to test disarray.

Dad packed up us kids and fled
the cheddar cubes, plastic forks suspended
in Jell-O—*that* was judgment, ambrosia and trident—

oh, but it was delicious
at the Drive-In, sliding in pajamas down
into the pit, waking

just in time to see
great Pharaoh drowned
and Charlton Heston rosy

in his holy rags . . . now, that
was a good story, that
kept us awake

until the end credits, the moon
huge as it wandered down
the black gullet of avenue,

bright eye swallowing
the windshield. . . . We made it
home to the ruins

of the feast: crustless sandwiches
smelling faintly of ocean, platoons
of celery, mints and dip (they always

finished the cake), a soggy lemon
crescent lolling in the red bottom
of the drained punch bowl,

and the house a mess. We ate like kings for days.

2. *CHARLTON HESTON'S HOLY RAGS*

Our lucky man puts in his first appearance.
We cheer, ski the front seat vinyl
into the plushy pit beneath the dash.

Just as sure as we're missing the chalky mints
discretely placed between the moistened lips
of the Reverend Sisters of the Eastern Star,

he'll save us from plopping frogs or locusts,
clouds of hissing *told-you-so*s
invading bed or pajama cuff.

This time around, though, he's neither
good nor wise: He tromps palatial corridors,
a smooth-cheeked boy in Roman bronze,

all greed and good looks.
No green smoke wriggling over a host of snakes
ready to be turned into walking sticks;

instead, he lifts his hand and an urn,
kicked, stutters across the tiles:
The car speaker crackles scorn.

What brand of righteousness is this? Squeamish,
we stuff our mouths with more buttered corn
and count the things gone wrong—

there's a sister rotting away in a cave,
too many sweaty people being whipped,
that skinny stranger's burning gaze . . .

and then, just when we begin to doubt him,
we watch as doubt struggles up to crouch
inside his own baby blues. Oh,

now he rises to his chiseled best,
takes redemption's arrow
deep into his manly chest

as rain comes down in torrents,
lightning timed to tell each flash of news
(the rock rolled back, the lepers' new-washed skin),

and through it all—the tears, the flood,
Thy Kingdom Come in gold
and cobalt streaks—he stands aglow

with Blessedness, with . . . could it be
remorse? Whatever for?—and in
an instant, he suddenly

grows old.

Meditation at Fifty Yards, Moving Target

Safety First.

Never point your weapon, keep your finger
off the trigger. Assume a loaded barrel,
even when it isn't, especially when you *know* it isn't.
Glocks are lightweight but sensitive;
the Keltec has a long pull and a kick.
Rifles have penetrating power, viz.:
if the projectile doesn't lodge in its mark,
it will travel some distance
until it finds shelter; it will certainly
pierce your ordinary drywall partition.
You could wound the burglar and kill your child
sleeping in the next room, all with one shot.

Open Air.

Fear, of course. Then the sudden
pleasure of heft—as if the hand
had always yearned for this solemn
fit, this *gravitas*, and now had found
its true repose.

Don't pull the trigger, squeeze it—
squeeze between heartbeats.
Look down the sights. Don't
hold your breath. Don't hold
anything, just stop breathing.
Level the scene with your eyes. Listen.
Soft, now: squeeze.

Gender Politics.

Guys like noise: rapid fire,
thunk-and-slide of a blunt-nose silver Mossberg,
or double-handed Colts, slugging it out from the hips.
Rambo or cowboy, they'll whoop it up.

Women are fewer, more elegant.
They prefer precision:
tin cans swing-dancing in the trees,
the paper bull's-eye's tidy rupture at fifty yards.

> (Question: If you were being pursued,
> how would you prefer to go down—
> ripped through a blanket of fire
> or plucked by one incandescent
> fingertip?)

The Bullet.

dark dark no wind no heaven
i am not anything not borne on air i bear
myself i can slice the air no wind
can hold me let me let me
go i can see yes
o aperture o light let me off
go off   straight is my verb straight
my glory road yes now i can feel
it the light i am flame velocity o
beautiful body i am coming i am yours
before you know it
i am home

American Smooth

We were dancing—it must have
been a foxtrot or a waltz,
something romantic but
requiring restraint,
rise and fall, precise
execution as we moved
into the next song without
stopping, two chests heaving
above a seven-league
stride—such perfect agony
one learns to smile through,
ecstatic mimicry
being the *sine qua non*
of American Smooth.
And because I was distracted
by the effort of
keeping my frame
(the leftward lean, head turned
just enough to gaze out
past your ear and always
smiling, smiling),
I didn't notice
how still you'd become until

we had done it
(for two measures?
four?)—achieved flight,
that swift and serene
magnificence,
before the earth
remembered who we were
and brought us down.

NOT WELCOME HERE

You may find nobility in the savage, Commander,
but he is only interested in killing you.

The Castle Walk

(*New York City, 1915. James Reese Europe, bandleader.*)

You can't accuse this group
of havin' too much mustard—
they're gloved and buttoned

tighter than Buddy's snare drum.
But they're paying, so
we pay 'em back—pour on

the violins, insinuate
a little cello,
lay some grizzly piano

under that sweet jelly roll.
Our boys got a snap and buzz
no one dancing

in this gauze and tinsel
showroom knows how
to hear: The couples stroll

past, counting to themselves
as they orbit, chins poked out
as if expecting a kiss or

in need of a shave; we pitch
and surge through each ragtime
and I swear, it's both

luck and hardship,
the way the music
slips as it burns.

These white folks stalk
through privilege
just like they dance:

one-two, stop, pose,
over and over.
We ain't nobody

special, but at least we know it:
Across the black Atlantic,
they're trampling up the map

into a crazy quilt of rage
and honor; here,
the biggest news going

would be Irene and Vernon
teaching the Castle Walk.
(Trot on, Irene! Vernon, fake that

juke joint slide.) So boys,
lay down tracks, the old world's
torched; we'll ride this train as far

as it's going. Let's kick it:
Time for the Innovation Tango!
Buddy, set 'em marching;

and you, Mr. Cricket Smith—mortify 'em
with your cornet's
molten silver moan!

The Passage

(*Corporal Orval E. Peyton,
372nd Infantry, 93rd Division, A.E.F.*)

Saturday, March 30, 1917

                                       Got up
this morning at 2:45, breakfast at 3:30,
a beautiful sky, warm, and the moon bright.
I slept in my clothes, overcoat and socks.
I was restless last night, listening to the others
moving about.

Now, all the boys seem cheerful.
This will be a day never to be forgotten.
After breakfast—beef stew and coffee—
Charlie and I cleaned up the rest of the mail.

             *   *   *

It is now 4:30 in the afternoon.
The whistle has blown for us
and everybody ordered down off deck.

I am not worried; I am anxious to go.

This morning we left camp at 7 and marched
silently along the town's perimeter to port.
No cheering nor tears shed, no one
to see us off, to kiss and cry over.
F company was leading. I looked back at
several hundred men
marching toward they knew not what.
When we passed through the lower end of the city
a few colored people
stood along the street, watching.
One lady raised her apron to wipe away a tear.

I turned my head to see how the fellow next to me,
Corporal Crawford from Massachusetts,
was taking it. Our eyes met and we both smiled.
Not that we thought it was funny, but—
we were soldiers.
There were more things in this world
than a woman's tears.

*　　*　　*

March 31

Easter Sunday.
I was up to services held by a chaplain
but am not feeling well enough to get something to eat.
All the boys are gathered around the hatch
singing "My Little Girl." Talked to a sailor
who's been across twice; he says this ship
has had four battles with subs, each time
beating them off.

This boat is named *The Susquehanna*—
German built, interned before
the U.S. declared war. Her old name was *The Rhine.*
The other ship that left Newport News with us
was known as *Prinz Friedrich.*

We pulled out last night at 5
and I soon went to bed, so tired
I nearly suffocated, for I had left off my fan.
(We sleep in bunks three high and two
side by side with no ventilation
in quarters situated near the steam room.
The stair straight down. Everything in steel.)

*　　*　　*

April 1 (All Fools' Day)

               Nothing but water.
Just back from breakfast, home-style:
sausage, potatoes and gravy, oatmeal, coffee, bread
and an apple. The food seems better here than
in camp. Our boys do not complain much.

The sailors say we are the jolliest bunch of fellows
they have ever taken across. This boat's been over
twice before and according to them
this trip is the charm—either
the ship will be sunk or it will be good for the war.
I guess we are bound to have trouble, for it is said
the submarines are busy in this kind of weather.

Last night I could not eat all my supper, so went on deck.
No moon out but the sky full of stars,
and I remember thinking
The future will always be with me.
About 7 o'clock I saw a few lights some distance ahead
a little to the left. The boat made toward them;
as we drew nearer I recognized a red beacon.
Our gunners got busy and trained the sights.

We passed within 500 yards.
The stern was all lit. Someone said
it was a hospital ship.

*　　*　　*

April 2, Tuesday

Good breakfast—
bacon, eggs, grits, and of course coffee.
We ran into ships ahead about an hour ago.
I can see four, probably the rest of the fleet.

Most of the boys are on deck. A few are down here
playing blackjack and poker, and the band's playing, too.
I've been on deck all morning, up on a beam
trying to read the semaphore.

5:30 p.m. Just had supper. We ate with F Company
tonight: potatoes, corned beef, apple butter and coffee.
We've overtaken the other ships; I can see four more
to our ports. I got wet on deck about an hour ago.

I can hear the waves splashing! I think
I'll go up and smoke before it gets dark.

*　　*　　*

April 3, Wednesday

Just came down
off deck; the sea is high and waves all over.
I put on my raincoat to get in them—great sport!
There were six ships to our ports and a battleship starboard.

4 p.m. The storm is rocking us so,
no one can stay on deck without getting soaked.
I have been in my bunk all afternoon.

Quite a few of the boys are sick by now.
I feel a trifle dizzy;
there's something wrong with the ship,
I don't know what it is, but they called for
all the pipe fitters they could find.
Some of the boys have put on life preservers
but most don't seem to be afraid and are as jolly
as if they were on shore. Some say
they don't think we'll make it.
We are some kind of circus down here.

*　　*　　*

7 p.m.: our ship gets a wireless every evening
telling us the war news. Ever since supper
there has been a bunch on deck laughing,
singing, and dancing. A large wave swept
over the planks and drenched us all but
the stronger the sea, the more noise we made.
At last, just as Pickney had finished
a mock speech with "I thank you, ladies and gentlemen,"
a larger wave poured a foot of water on deck.

The sailors had crowded around us; they say
pity the Germans when a bunch like us hit them.

*   *   *

April 4, Thursday

                    Fifth day out.
I'm feeling all right—that is,
I don't feel like I did when I was on land,
but I am not sick. Last night I couldn't go to sleep
for a long while in that hot hole.
About 4 a.m., I put on my slippers
and went up for a breath of air.
The storm had passed and stars were shining,
half a dozen sailors busy with ropes.

One of the guards instructed me to close
my slicker, for my white underclothes were glowing.

Everybody this morning was in good spirits
and the deck was crowded with our boys.
Calm sea, a fair breeze blowing.
At ten o'clock we had "Abandon Ship" drill:
we were ordered below to our bunks
to put on life preservers, then
a whistle blew, some petty officers yelled
"all hands abandon ship," and we went
quickly to our places on the raft.
There are twenty-five of us in a boat.
My boat's number one.

                    *   *   *

When I think that I am a thousand miles
from land, in the middle of the Ocean,
I am not a bit impressed as I imagined I would be.
Things have certainly changed. A year ago
I was sitting in school, studying.
I had never been out of the state of Ohio
and never gone from home for more than
two weeks at a time. Now I'm away

eight months—four in the Deep South,
four in Virginia and now
on the High Seas.
I wonder where I'll be this time next year.

*   *   *

April 5, Friday

                        Last night after dinner
I started reading a book borrowed from Crawford
titled *Life of the Immortal.* Stopped
long enough for supper, and finished it
about an hour ago. Then with Shelton,
Davis, and Crawford, talked about literature.
I didn't get to bed before 10 o'clock
and did not feel like getting up this morning.

It is very hard to obtain soap on board
that will lather in salt water.
I can't get my hands clean without soap; but
one of the sailors gave me a piece
that's pretty good. So far I have managed
to stay fresh but some of the dudes don't care
and their hands are awful looking.
I haven't shaved since I've been

on board; I won't shave
until land is in sight.

✳   ✳   ✳

April 6, Saturday

Wrestling match
with Casey; I was wet with sweat when we stopped
and went on deck to cool off.
We're served just two meals a day now, 9 and 3 o'clock.
Rich Tuggle and others bought a lot of cakes and candy
from the canteen, so I was too full to eat supper.

This morning in the mess line
Rick spotted some kind of large fish near our boat.
All I saw was its tail, but it shot up water
like I've seen in pictures in school.

A whale, I thought, *maybe it's a whale!*
But it went under without a noise.

✳   ✳   ✳

April 7, Sunday

           We had a death
on board last night, a cook by the name of Bibbie.
Chaplain Nelson held the service
on the other end of the boat.
Mess call sounded before he had finished.
(Pork, potatoes, corn and coffee.)

This is an ideal Sunday afternoon;
I wonder what we would be doing back home
if I was there. Now I will read awhile
and then lie down. I am tired of the voyage.
I suppose there are lonesome days before me,
but no more so than those that have already passed.
I can make myself contented.
We are having very good weather.

It must have been a whale!

Noble Sissle's Horn

(Northern France/Spartansburg, South Carolina.
The 369th.)

A cornet's soul is in its bell—
trap that liquid gasp
and you're cooking.

> *(Take your hat off, boy.*
> *Not quick enough.*
> *Pick it up! Too slow.)*

A horn needs to choke on
what feeds it, it has to want
the air to sing out.

> *Nigger, where you been raised?*
> *This is a respectable establishment.*

The difference between a moan and a hallelujah
ain't much of a slide.
I don't know how I knew this,
growing up deep in the church
deep in Indianapolis—

Bent over like a mule
from one bitty kick—why,
you need strengthening.

but right now, standing here itching
up under all this wool, I figure:

What you staring at?
You got something to say?

When you've got whole nations lining up
just to mow each other down—hell,
a man can hoot just as well as holler.

Alfonzo Prepares to Go Over the Top

(Belleau Wood, 1917)

"A soldier waits until he's called—then
moves ass and balls up, over
tearing twigs and crushed faces,
swinging his bayonet like a pitchfork
and thinking *anything's better*
than a trench, ratshit
and the tender hairs of chickweed.
A soldier is smoke
waiting for wind; he's a long corridor
clanging to the back of a house
where a child sings
in its ruined nursery. . .
          and Beauty is the
gleam of my eye on this gunstock and my spit
drying on the blade of this knife
before it warms itself in the gut of a Kraut.
Mother, forgive me. Hear the leaves? I am
already memory."

La Chapelle. 92nd Division. Ted.

(September, 1918)

This lonely beautiful word
                            means church
and it is quiet here; the stone
walls curve
                  like slow water.
When we arrived the people were already gone,
green shutters latched and stoops swept clean.
A cow lowed through the village,
pushing into our gloves her huge
sodden jaw.

It's Sunday and I'm standing
on the bitter ridge of France, overlooking the war.
La Guerre is asleep. This morning early
on patrol we slipped down through
the mist and scent of burning woodchips
(somewhere someone was warm)
                                    into Moyenmoutier,
cloister of flushed brick and a little river
braiding its dark hair.

Back home in Louisiana the earth is red,
but it suckles you until you can sing
yourself grown.
                     Here, even the wind has edges.
Drizzle splintered around us; we stood
on the arched bridge and thought
for a moment of the dead we had left
behind in the valley, in the terrible noise.

But I'm not sad—on the way back
through the twigs I glimpsed
in a broken windowbox by the roadside
mums:
stunned lavenders and pinks
dusted with soot.
                     I am a little like them,
heavy-headed,
rough curls open to the rain.

Variation on Reclamation

(Aix-les-Bains. 1918. Teddy.)

Coming To.

    Music across the lake? Impossible . . .
    it had to be coming from behind him,
    doughboys in the square, catching some rays,

    Calvin's piccolo tickling the air.
    He'd let it ride, just a little while . . .

2nd Waking.

    Every morning tap-step, tap-step
    from cot to veranda, then lean

    against the doorframe, head back
    to feel the dew. *All right: Ready?*

    Elbow cocked (*yes*) to push
    the forearm through the sleeve

    (*check*), jacket hunched up and
    over (*hoopla!*)—to do at least

this much!—brought tears. *Good work,*
they'd say; why don't you rest a bit?

For the walk back, they mean.
The sun on his cheek, a gentle burn.

Setback. Bedrest.
How could he recover without a song?
His whistle tuckered, voice cracked
into a thousand rasps and throttles.

No tin cup, but here's a hook to keep him
in line—silver curve too ornery

to strum or take bets with,
lift a caramel chin for a kiss . . .

Dismissal.
He'd been to the mountain
and found it green and trembling

with its fallen. He'd called out
so many times to those lost last breaths

it was like listening to his own heart
—flutter, stop, kick, canter—

all in a day's climb. The stick
wasn't there for decoration:

he'd own it, old man tottering
out of hellfire, a medal bumping

his chest (*step, tap*), at his back
an impertinent nation

popping gum as they jeered: *Boy,*
we told you to watch your step.

The Return of Lieutenant James Reese Europe

(Victory Parade, New York City, February 1919.)

We trained in the streets: the streets where we came from.
We drilled with sticks, boys darting between bushes, shouting—
that's all you thought we were good for. We trained anyway.
In camp we had no plates or forks. First to sail, first to
    join the French,
first to see combat with the shortest training time.

My, the sun is looking fine today.

We toured devastation, American good will
in a forty-four piece band. Dignitaries smiled; the wounded
settled back to dream. That old woman in St. Nazaire
who tucked up her skirts so she could "walk the dog."
German prisoners tapping their feet as we went by.

Miss Flatiron with your tall cool self: How do.

You didn't want us when we left but we went.
You didn't want us coming back but here we are,
stepping right up white-faced Fifth Avenue in a phalanx
(*no prancing, no showing of teeth, no swank*)
past the Library lions, eyes forward, tin hats aligned—

a massive, upheld human shield.

No jazz for you: We'll play a brisk French march
and show our ribbons, flash our *Croix de Guerre*
(yes, we learned French, too) all the way
until we reach 110th Street and yes! take our turn
onto Lenox Avenue and all those brown faces and then—

Baby, Here Comes Your Daddy Now!

Ripont

The men helped clear the enemy out of Bussy Farm,
advanced toward Ripont, and were in the fighting at Sechault;
then they were pulled back to Bussy Farm. In these actions
they captured sixty of the enemy, and equipment including
several artillery and antitank weapons.

Early fall in the fields a slow day's drive south
of Paris French birds singing frenchly enough
though we didn't know their names in any language—
not even the German of my husband
reared in a village like the one we were passing
in our rusty orange BMW   baby daughter
crowing from the backseat her plastic shell
strapped over the cracked upholstery

We were *en route* to the battlefields of the 369th
the Great War's Negro Soldiers
who it was said fought like tigers
joking as the shells fell around them
so that the French told the Americans
Send us more like these and they did and so
the Harlem Hellfighters earned their stripes
in the War To End All Wars

We followed cow paths bisected pastures
barreled down stretches of gravel arrow straight
until the inevitable curve signaling each hamlet

noonday silence dreary stone barns and a few
crooked houses cobblestones boiling up
under our wheels the air thick with flies
the sky streaked cream stirred in a cup

The maps we'd bought in Montparnasse were exquisite
Each dry creek bed and fallow square
each warped stile or cracked fountain appeared
at the appointed millimeter under my index finger
This afternoon the battlefield at Ripont
one more name in a string of villages
destroyed during the course of their own salvation
We were thrilled when the copse of oaks
appeared on the left just as the five dots printed
in the crease of the Michelin had predicted
we counted the real trees to see if there were five
of them too but there were seven   Down an embankment

then to the blue squiggle denoting a stream
our daughter gurgling her pleasure as I reached back
to feed her another spoonful of Gerber's spinach
cold from the jar   A sharp right
onto the map's dotted line   Two tire tracks
leading into deeper foliage path blotted by vines
the sun a cottony blur too far off to help us

through locked branches a sudden rectangle yellow and black
Achtung - Minen   watch out for mines

This was the village before that September
decades ago before victory ploughed through
leaving her precocious seeds   Past
the brambles the broken staves of barbed wire
we could see a frayed doorway a keystone
frame of a house gone a-kilter
like a child's smudged crayon drawing

A branch slapped the windshield I shrieked
rolled up the windows as if tragedy were
contagious as if our daughter could detonate
the mines by tossing her rattle into the briars
We were in deep no way out except by
shifting in reverse so we drove on till at last
there came a clearing a crabgrass mound
choked under a layer of gleaming automobiles

Nothing to do but park so we pulled behind
a Peugeot got out and followed the road
on foot turning a bend onto a smattering
of people decked out in their somber best
some older ladies with corsages some with veils
a lean man with the hat and mustache of a mayor

was giving a speech   We made out
the year of the battle the name of the town
a bugle sounded as two old soldiers laid down a wreath
and only then did we notice the memorial stone
with the date   today's   and the names of the fallen
both the French and the Negro

Everyone smiled at us sadly they thought
we were descendants too
What else could we do we smiled back
we let them believe we drove with the crowd
single file through the woods to the river
where we turned left they turned right
some of them waving
our daughter waving back
We kept on until twilight stopped us
found an inn in a town not starred on our map
where I sat in a room at a small wooden table
by the side of our bed and wrote nothing
for thirteen years not a word in my notebook
until today

for Aviva, leaving home

TWELVE CHAIRS

My logic was not in error, but I was.

First Juror

Proof casts a shadow;
doubt is to walk
onto a field
at high noon
one tendril
held to
the
wind.

Second Juror

A stone to throw

A curse to hurl

A silence to break

A page to write

A day to live

A blank

To fill

Third Juror

between the lip
and the kiss
between the hand
and the fist
between rumor
and prayer
between dungeon
and tower
between fear
and liberty
always
between

Fourth Juror

Cancel the afternoon
evenings mornings all
the days to come
until the fires
fall to ash
the fog clears
and we can see
where we
really
stand.

Fifth Juror

How long will
this take?
I am not my
brother,
thank you;
my hands are
full already
taking care
of
myself.

Sixth Juror

I'm not anyone more
than anyone else.
I did my job, then
looked into
their eyes.
What had I
become?

Seventh Juror

In the mind of the crow
burns a golden cry In
the heart of the mole
an endless sky In
the eye of the trout
shines a galaxy
And I who see this
tell no one
I who am
a corridor
longing
to be
field

Eighth Juror

Look around:
magic everywhere.
Behind you,
tears and shadow.
Ahead the path
clean flame.
Look up, the air
is singing:
Underfoot
your shadow
waits.

Ninth Juror

Not the eyes—never
look into the eyes.
The soul either
strikes out
or
trembles
beneath
the blow.

Tenth Juror

Tragedy
involves
one.
History
involves many
toppling
one
after
another.

Eleventh Juror

You can't mop the floor
before the milk's
been spilled;
you can't run off
if your shadow
is pinned
to
the wall.

Twelfth Juror

why is the rose
how is the sun
where is first
when is last
who will
love us
what
will
save
us

The Alternate

—And who are you?
　　—*Nobody.*
—What do you do?
　　—*I am alive.*
—But who'll vouch
　　for you?
　　—*Listen closely,*
　　　you'll hear
　　　　the
　　　wind.

BLUES IN HALF-TONES, 3/4 TIME

[Our] heart was forged out of barbarism
and violence. We learned to control it,
but it is still a part of us. To pretend it
does not exist is to create an opportunity
for it to escape.

Chocolate

Velvet fruit, exquisite square
I hold up to sniff
between finger and thumb—

how you numb me
with your rich attentions!
If I don't eat you quickly,

you'll melt in my palm.
Pleasure seeker, if I let you
you'd liquefy everywhere.

Knotted smoke, dark punch
of earth and night and leaf,
for a taste of you

any woman would gladly
crumble to ruin.
Enough chatter: I am ready

to fall in love!

Bolero

Not the ratcheting crescendo of Ravel's bright winds
but an older,
crueler

passion: a woman with hips who knows when to move them,
who holds nothing back
but the hurt

she takes with her as she dips, grinds, then rises sweetly into
his arms again.
Not

delicate. Not tame. Bessie Smith in a dream of younger,
(*Can't you see?*)
slimmer

days. Restrained in the way a debutante is not, the way a bride
pretends she
understands.

How everything hurts! Each upsurge onto a throbbing toe,
the prolonged descent
to earth,

to him (*what love & heartache done to me*), her body ferocious,
a grim ululation
of flesh—

she adores him. And he savors that adoration, this man in love
                                                    with looking.
She feels his look,
his sigh

and she moves, moves with him to the music in the space
                                                    allotted them,
spot lit across
the hardwood floor.

Hattie McDaniel Arrives at the Coconut Grove

late, in aqua and ermine, gardenias
scaling her left sleeve in a spasm of scent,
her gloves white, her smile chastened, purse giddy
with stars and rhinestones clipped to her brilliantined hair,
on her free arm that fine Negro,
Mr. Wonderful Smith.

It's the day that isn't, February 29th,
at the end of the shortest month of the year—
and the shittiest, too, everywhere
except Hollywood, California,
where the maid can wear mink and still be a maid,
bobbing her bandaged head and cursing
the white folks under her breath as she smiles
and shoos their silly daughters
in from the night dew . . . what can she be
thinking of, striding into the ballroom
where no black face has ever showed itself
except above a serving tray?

Hi-Hat Hattie, Mama Mac, Her Haughtiness,
the "little lady" from *Showboat* whose name
Bing forgot, Beulah & Bertha & Malena
& Carrie & Violet & Cynthia & Fidelia,
one half of the Dark Barrymores—

dear Mammy we can't help but hug you crawl into
your generous lap tease you
with arch innuendo so we can feel that
much more wicked and youthful
and sleek but oh what

we forgot: the four husbands, the phantom
pregnancy, your famous parties, your celebrated
ice box cake. Your giggle above the red petticoat's rustle,
black girl and white girl walking hand in hand
down the railroad tracks
in Kansas City, six years old.
The man who advised you, now
that you were famous, to "begin eliminating"
your more "common" acquaintances
and your reply (catching him square
in the eye): "That's a good idea.
I'll start right now by eliminating you."

Is she or isn't she? Three million dishes,
a truckload of aprons and headrags later, and here
you are: poised, between husbands
and factions, no corset wide enough
to hold you in, your huge face a dark moon split
by that spontaneous smile—your trademark,

your curse. No matter, Hattie: It's a long, beautiful walk
into that flower-smothered standing ovation,
so go on
and make them wait.

Samba Summer

Fort Valley, Georgia, 1966

Broke-leg cakewalk of the drunken uncles
entertaining the ladies at the family picnic:
one arm akimbo in a humpback strut,
the other stretched high in witness—*yes, Lord, yes!*—
palm outspread against a late summer sky.

> *That skirt's too yellow*
> *and far too tight*
> *for any Christian child.*
> *I'd walk a mile*
> *if the gal was right*
> *but those hips could kill a fellow!*

One straight leg, too, that the crooked one dragged
through a grassy rut edging the petunias.
The women rolled their eyes, clucked
the children away from the charred hibachi,
and set out the coconut cream pies.

> *You may as well*
> *go on and shoot me,*
> *tie my heart in a knot.*
> *Wait: judging from*
> *this limp here,*
> *my leg's already shot!*

High-butt shenanigans! Uncles did it best,
pot-gutted, hitching their trousers up—
a holy grunting executed to the bleat and hiss
of Mitzi's seafoam green transistor,
comic signature of the tribe:

> We're only joking: we know
> we're just the world's
> custodians, full-time lovers
> on half pay. C'mon, girl,
> let's dance—before this song is over,
> show me what I've been working for.

Blues in Half-Tones, 3/4 Time

From nothing comes nothing,
don't you know that by now?
Not a thing for you, sweet thing,
not a wing nor a prayer,
though you got half
by birthright,
itching under the skin.

(There's a typo somewhere.)
Buck 'n' wing,
common prayer—
which way do you run?
The oaken bucket's
all busted
and the water's all gone.

I'm not for sale because I'm free.
(So they say. They say
the play's the thing, too,
but we *know* that don't play.)
Everyone's a ticket
or a stub, so it might as well
cost you, my dear.

But are you sure you lost it?
Did you check the back seat?
What a bitch. Gee, that sucks.
Well, you know what they say.
What's gone's gone.
No use crying.
(There's a moral *somewhere*.)

Describe Yourself in Three Words or Less

I'm not the kind of person who praises
openly, or for profit; I'm not the kind
who will steal a scene unless
I've designed it. I'm not a kind at all,
in fact: I'm itchy and pug-willed,
gnarled and wrong-headed,
never amorous but possessing
a wild, thatched soul.

Each night I set my boats to sea
and leave them to their bawdy business.
Whether they drift off
maddened, moon-rinsed,
or dock in the morning
scuffed and chastened—
is simply how it is, and I gather them in.

You are mine, I say to the twice-dunked cruller
before I eat it. Then I sing
to the bright-beaked bird outside,
then to the manicured spider
between window and screen;
then I will stop, and forget the singing.
(See? I have already forgotten you.)

The Seven Veils of Salomé

Salomé Awaits Her Entrance.

> I was standing in the doorway
> when he reproached her.
> Not with words, but a simple
> absence of attention: She was smiling,
> holding out a slip of meat, skewered fruit—
> some delicacy he'd surely never seen
> in all his dust-blown, flea-plagued
> wanderings—and he stared at it
> for the longest while,
> as if the offer came from it and not
> those tapered fingers, my mother's
> famous smile. He said nothing,
> merely turned away his large
> and beautifully arrogant head.

Herodias, in the Doorway.

> More than anything I ache to see her
> so girlish. She steps languidly
> into their midst as if onto a pooled expanse
> of grass . . . or as if she were herself
> the meadow, unruffled green
> ringed with lilies

instead of these red-rimmed eyes,
this wasteland soaked in smoke and pleasure.
Ignorant, she moves as if inventing
time—and the musicians scurry
to deliver a carpet of flutes
under her flawless heel.

Herod, Watching.

I should have avoided this, loving her mother
as I do, to the length and breadth of my kingdom,
even to the chilly depths of history's wrath.
But it was my birthday; I was bent upon
happiness and love, I loved
Herodias, my Herodias!—who sends
her honeyed daughter into the feast.
The first veil fell, and all
my celebrated years
dissolved in bitter rapture. O Herodias!
You have outdone us all.

The Fool, at Herod's Feet.

> Just a girl, slim-hipped, two knots
> for breasts, sheathed potential
> caught before the inevitable
> over-bloom and rot (life's revenge
> if death eludes us)—all
> any of us men want, really.
> Just a girl. Otherwise,
> who can fathom it, how is it
> to be fathomed? At his behest, her mother's?
> It matters little—she was dispatched
> into the circle of elders, and there
> she rivets the world's desire.

Salomé, Dancing.

> I have a head on my shoulders
> but no one sees it; no one
> reckons with a calculated wrist or pouting underlip.
> I've navigated this court's attentions
> and I will prove I can be crueler than government,
> I will delegate what nature's given me
> (this body, this anguish,
> oiled curves and perfumed apertures),

I will dance until they've all lost their heads—
the nobles slobbering over their golden goblets,
the old king sweating on his throne,
my mother in the doorway, rigid with regret,
the jester who watches us all and laughs—

O Mother, what else is a girl to do?

From Your Valentine

(Valentinus, imprisoned.)

The days pass. Night floats,
continuous, a dark sheen in terror's
velvet grip. Is this what you
live in, dearest blind girl,
my jailor's daughter?
Like a shell whose portion of ocean
is constantly rocking,
keeping time, you carry
the cell of yourself
quietly. How else to locate
the anger in a tongue's *chk chk*,
the swift bite of his keys before
his hand slices the air? Outside

the city shouts, it growls and throbs.
You bring its hunger back
to whisper in my ear
and I write it down, ears burning—
all that pierced, burst, suppurating
anguish rendered into words,
hopeless scraps you slip
under your skirts, unabashed,
baring a thigh you cannot see.

Yet this sight does not stir me;
God's will is shameless. Only when
darkness swallows and you are all
around me and inside the dark—
O then I am most alive, spitted and turning,
and I dread . . . not pain,
snug in its own embrace, not
being without you, since I am
alone already—but the moment
before death, when pain and absence
blur, when I'll become
pure sensation.

I am calm when I can hear
your approach; I feel you
listening for me, my breathing
measured to your hurried step.
And when I speak, you lift
your entire body
into my voice, and I can look at you
all I want—I sin
over and over in gluttonous gazing,
your careful and thirsty face
a mirror
to my own. O my heart

is vigilant, hardened
to a single point it spins upon.
Martyrdom is easy:
I'll take the coward's path
and insist upon
my God, my righteous
love . . . until that love
snuffs out the man before you,
the one you see clearly,
who lives now
for the first time.

Rhumba

yo vengo aquí   I come here
para cantar   to sing
la rumba   the rumba
de mi adoración   of my adoration

Wait.

                  Here comes

At his touch

                the music:

(just under the tricep)

            lean back, look at me—

lock your knees,

             the straighter your legs

look, straight up

             the easier to fall,

into him, his hand stroking

               to descend

your cheek . . . .

                 lightly.

Don't close your eyes.

            Don't bend your knees.

Let the body lift you

          Sigh upwards—trust me!

back on your feet.

               Wait. Now

A touch again:

                      dip down

this time, twist

                   but spread your arms;

in the knees,

                   give me some tone

but soft, follow (soft)

                      (more tone)

the reach, that last yearning

                   & connect . . . .

to his left wrist.

                Where's the audience?

Step forward.

                    Find them.

Rondé-hook-turn

               Let them see your face;

& reach again,

                now look for the stars,

reach, reach then

                     yes, keep

snap back—

                your elbow straight!

back to him,

                   Here I am, &

always back to him . . . .

here's your basic walk:

Ah, hips.

Enjoy it.

Quick-&-quick-

Hear the music? Enjoy it.

& slow . . .

Remember,

snake the right arm up,

after every turn

rock back &

find me &

dive, a swan,

shape,

head in the clouds

shoulders down—

then drop left,

keep going,

he'll catch you,

I've got you—

(good) to a right foot

quick quick now

slow:

relax.

Shape right,

        Here comes the spiral;

kick back,

          let me lead it.

yearn over him

        C'mon, milk it, turn

to meet his thigh,

         easy, easy . . .

ripple up his back.

          don't settle.

Repeat on the left side.

         Here's the check:

(Whew! That's over.)

         beautiful line.

Rondé, pose:

        Keep it tight, turn

quick-&-quick

        (let me lead you)

knee up over &

       —look at me,

lean, unwind & melt

        find my eyes

toward him

       so we can turn away

(straight legs) no—

                            in sync. & finally,

resist: *embrace:*

          my right your left
          my left your right
          your left his right
          your right his left

(don't cross your eyes)

                  look at me look deep

half spin to the right

                 forget the audience

stay on your toes now

                 lean into me,

define the length of him . . .

                 that's right . . .

the audience

                 forget them

the audience

                 your body

shuddering

                 all mine

into applause

                 now

The Sisters: Swansong.

We died one by one,
each plumper than the mirror
saw us. We exited obligingly,
rattling key chains and
cocktail jewelry, rehearsing
our ghostly encores.

Glad to be rid of pincurls
and prayers, bunions
burning between
ironed sheets—we sang
our laments, praised God
and went our way

quietly, were mourned
in satin and chrysanthemums,
whiskey and cake, old gossip
evaporating into cautionary tales.
Does it matter who went
first? Corinna or Fay,

heartache or coronary,
a reckless scalpel or
a careless life—whoever was left
kept count on the dwindling
rosary: Suzanna, Kit.
Mary. Violet. Pearl.

We all died of insignificance.

EVENING PRIMROSE

Proceed . . . carefully.

Evening Primrose

Poetically speaking, growing up is mediocrity.
—Ned Rorem

Neither rosy nor prim,
not cousin to the cowslip
nor the extravagant fuchsia—
I doubt anyone has ever
picked one for show,
though the woods must be fringed
with their lemony effusions.

Sun blathers its baronial
endorsement, but they refuse
to join the ranks. Summer
brings them in armfuls,
yet, when the day is large,
you won't see them fluttering
the length of the road.

They'll wait until the world's
tucked in and the sky's
one ceaseless shimmer—then
lift their saturated eyelids
and blaze, blaze
all night long
for no one.

Reverie in Open Air

I acknowledge my status as a stranger:
Inappropriate clothes, odd habits
Out of sync with wasp and wren.
I admit I don't know how
To sit still or move without purpose.
I prefer books to moonlight, statuary to trees.

But this lawn has been leveled for looking,
So I kick off my sandals and walk its cool green.
Who claims we're mere muscle and fluids?
My feet are the primitives here.
As for the rest—ah, the air now
Is a tonic of absence, bearing nothing
But news of a breeze.

Sic Itur Ad Astra

Thus is the way to the stars.
—Virgil

Bed, where are you flying to?
I went to sleep
nearly an hour ago,
and now I'm on a porch
open to the stars!

Close my eyes
and sink back to
day's tiny dismissals;
open wide and I'm
barefoot, nightshirt
fluttering white as a sail.

What will they say
when they find me
missing—just
the shape of my dreaming
creasing the sheets?
Come here, bed,

I need you! I don't know my way.
At least leave my pillow
behind to remind me
what affliction I've fled—
my poor, crushed pillow

with its garden of smells!

Count to Ten and We'll Be There

One chimpanzee.
Two crocodiles.
Three kings and a star make
Four . . . my new shoe size, just
Five days old. (I'm twice that now.) It's June—
Six more months until snow for sure.
Seven was lucky, not like
Eight, when I got glasses, better than
Nine, which felt Egyptian.

I'm ten now, which ends in
Zero. I've got
Four grandparents,
Three siblings,
Two parents and
One head with
Nothing to look at,
No place else to go.

Eliza, Age 10, Harlem

I'm not small like they say,
those withered onions on the stoop
clucking their sorrowful tongues.
I'm concentrated. I'm a sweet
package of love. Jesus

says so, and He's better than angels
'cause He knows how to die;
He suffers the children
to come unto Him.
I can climb these stairs—

easy, even in T-straps. Yes,
I am my grandma's sugar pea
and someday I'm gonna pop
right out—and then, boys,
you better jump back!

Lullaby

(after Lorca's "Canción Tonta")

Mother, I want to rest in your lap again
as I did as a child.

Put your head here. How it floats,
heavy as your whole body was once.

If I fall asleep, I will be stiff
when I awake.

No stiffer than I.

But I want to lie down and do nothing
forever.

When I was angry with your father, I would take to my bed
like those fainting Victorian ladies.

I'm not angry at anyone.
Mostly I'm bored.

Boredom is useful for embroidery,
and a day of rest never hurt anyone.

Mother, I want the birthday supper of my childhood,
dripping with sauce.

Then you must lie down while I fix it!
Here, a pillow for your back.

I can't. The school bus is coming.
She'll be waiting at the corner.

Already? So soon!

Driving Through

I know this scene: There's an engine
idling, without keys, just outside Mr. Nehi's
algebra class. I escape without notice,
past the frosted glass of the wood shop
and the ironclad lockers with their inscrutable hasps
that never shut clean. I know
the sweet hum of tires over asphalt,
green tunnels trickling sun,
proud elmfire before Dutch blight
vacuumed the corridors bare. And the rowdy kids
cluttering the curb, nappy heads bobbing,
squirrel blood streaking their sharpened sticks—
I know them, too. After all, this is the past
I'm driving through, and I know I'll end up
where I started, stiff-necked and dull-hearted,
cursing last night's red wine. So when

this girl, this woman-of-a-child
with her cheap hoops and barnyard breasts
snatches the door and flops onto the vinyl shouting
Let's ride!, I nod and head straight for
the police, although I can't quite recall
where the station is, law enforcement
not being part of my past.
Run me home first, she barks,

smiling, enjoying the bluff:
I need my good earrings.
I tell her we're almost there, which
we aren't, not by half, and how would I know
where she lives, anyway? We're both smiling
now; but only when we're good and lost,
traffic thinned to no more than

a mirage of flayed brick and scorched cement,
does she blurt out: *You're lying.*
True, I think; but lying is what I do best.
I turn toward her, meaning to confess
my wild affliction, my art. Instead
I hiss gibberish; she panics,
slams the door handle down and hurls

her ripe body into the street where
no one will ever remember seeing her
again.
                    What was that?
My husband bolts up from his pillow.
Just a dream, I stammer, head pounding
as I try to fall asleep again—
even though I knew that girl was lost
long before I went back to find her.

Desert Backyard

Argentinean Pampas grass slices the careless ankle easily
and stings three days, most ardently at night.
Peruvian mulberry beguiles us
with purple pods called *pochettes d'amour:*
plump satchels that attack the heart.
The pear will not bear fruit; each spring
she stands arrayed in lace until
heat and wind bring that white affair

shamelessly down. We trim Egyptian sea grass
along the stone embrasure, prop up
flatulent elephant ears with sticks.
(Starved into vagrancy, the roses weep
gnawed petals.) The oleander, of course,
refuses to die. Burned in alleyways,
its sharp smoke cloys and raises welts,
fevered pockets of love leeched from the air.
Nowhere a delicacy, a pittance:

O deliver us
from magnificence.

Desk Dreams

Tempe, Arizona

Honeyed wood with one eye widening the grain
just above my migratory pen.
I love this unconscious solitude—

the way whole afternoons belong to the cicada
calling down to her cousins
in yellow Mexico.

Paris, France

Janis on the radio, nonstop blues.
Midnight traffic from Gare du Nord,
surge and ebb of taxis and vegetable trucks
wafting through three stories of rain.
Places to get to. On the black desk
a full palette of notebooks
offering up their moonlit pages.

Research Triangle Park, North Carolina

White-bricked cell. One leafy, appreciative plant.
General issue desk and a balcony
leading nowhere, though the eye travels
deep into androgynous green.

Blue-ruled paper from grade school days.
I languish for hours
on the near side of a hyphen: great expectations
cut by the call
of a single prehensile jay.

Bellagio, Italy

Not a studio so much as an earthbound turret,
or a periscope thrust
through the earth's omphalos:

Yoo-hoo, anybody there?
The walls are sleek as a shell's.

I will write my way out on a spiral of poems.
A mile down waits the lake,
chill Cyclopean blue;

while outside the door glimmers
the lesser mirror

of an artificial pond.
Is it true goldfish grow
to fit their containers?

Circles within circles:
Rapunzel, let down your hair.

Charlottesville, Virginia

Under crashed rafters
you stand,
honey in the ashes.

Your soaked plywood
and crazed veneer
aren't even worth

the hourly wage
of these men
in blue shirts

building boxes,
Salvage Experts trained
in the packing and storage

of household effects
singed by adversity,
anointed by the fireman's hose.

I save you by begging
sentimentality:
a female prerogative

I am grateful this once
to claim, since
tears will not serve

on a day as blue
as this one, the heavens
scrubbed and shining.

Now

The glass shone cold
with water fresh

from somebody's old
"family spring" west

of the Blue Ridge.
I drank half

in one continuous
gulp—not

greed, but because
the day was hot.

Then, out of breath or
the telephone

rang, I don't remember—
I stopped. I put the glass down

to mist on the counter
as I warmed to whatever

errand required my
sensibilities.

I was gone
all day

and when I returned, there
it stood—forgotten, slippery

in a darkening
ring

of neglect—mute evidence
of my earlier thirst

now room temperature,
one half of pure

nothing. No small
task, then

to reach for the glass and
drink it all.

Against Flight

Everyone wants to go up—but no one can imagine
what it's like when the earth smoothes out, begins

to curve into its own implacable symbol.
Once you've adjusted to chilled footsoles,

what to do with your hands? Can so much wind
be comfortable? No sense

looking around when you can see
everywhere: There'll be no more clouds

worth reshaping into daydreams, no more
daybreaks to make you feel larger than life;

no eagle envy or fidgeting for a better view
from the eighteenth row in the theater . . .

no more theatre, for that matter, and no
concerts, no opera or ballet. There'll be

no distractions except birds,
who never look you straight in the face,

and at the lower altitudes,
monarch butterflies—brilliant genetic engines

churning toward resurrection in a foreign land.
Who needs it? Each evening finds you

whipped to fringes, obliged to lie down
in a world of strangers, beyond perdition or pity—

bare to the stars, buoyant in the sweet sink of earth.

Looking Up from the Page, I Am Reminded
of This Mortal Coil

Mercurial ribbon licking the cut lip of the Blue Ridge—
    daybreak
        or end, I can't tell
as long as I ignore the body's marching orders, as long as
        I am alive in air . . .

What good is the brain without traveling shoes?
We put our thoughts out there on the cosmos express
    and they hurtle on, tired and frightened,
        bundled up in their worrisome
           shawls and gloves—I'm just

guessing here, but I suspect we don't
    travel easily at all, though we keep
    making better wheels—
        smaller phones and wider webs,
        ye olde significant glance
           across the half-empty goblet
           of Chardonnay. . . .

The blaze freshens,
        five or six miniature birds
        strike up the band.
Daybreak, of course; no more strobe and pink gels
        from the heavenly paint shop: just
house lights, play's over, time to gather your things and go home.

The New York Public Library
High Bridge Branch
08 SEP 2006 04:17pm
78 West 168th Street
(718) 293-7800
www.nypl.org

Checkout

American smooth :
3333184983035   Due: 29 SEP 2006 *

Return items to any NYPL branch in
the Bronx, Manhattan, or Staten Island.
Fines will be charged on overdue items.
Review and renew on-loan titles
on LEOLine at (212) 262-7444
or via the Web at
http://leopac.nypl.org

LEOLine and Internet renewal service is
not available if you have any of these:
  — 3 or more items overdue
  — fines of more than $10
  — any item 30 days overdue

NOTES

FRONTISPIECE: The definitions of "American" and "smooth" are excerpted from *The American Heritage Dictionary of the English Language,* 3rd and 4th editions (Houghton Mifflin). The definition of "American Smooth" is my own.

"QUICK," "BROWN," "FOX": *The quick brown fox jumped over the lazy dog.* This sentence, which contains all the letters in the English alphabet and has been the delight of countless school children and the despair of many typists-in-training, was my inspiration for a multimedia piece that was auctioned at a gala benefiting the Virginia Center for the Creative Arts (VCCA) during the Foxfield Races in Charlottesville, Virginia, in 2002: a painted plywood fox, the words "Quick Brown Fox" parading along his arched spine, carried the three poems you see here: one rolled into his collar, one tucked into a saddlebag, one in a pouch tied to his tail.

"SOPRANO" is dedicated to Edmund Najera.

"MEDITATION AT FIFTY YARDS, MOVING TARGET" is dedicated to Gabriel Robins.

NOT WELCOME HERE: African-Americans clamoring to enlist for combat during World War I came up against the bulwark of Race: The American armed forces, segregated and intransigent, showed no trust in the combat-worthiness of the would-be soldiers, who languished stateside until the French, who knew no such squeamishness, asked for them. The celebrated 369th was the first regiment to arrive; by war's end, it had logged the longest time in continuous combat (191 days) and received a staggering number of medals (170 individual Croix de Guerre). It was also the first regiment to fight its way to the Rhine in 1918.

Grateful acknowledgment is made to two sources in particular: *Scott's Official History of the American Negro in the World War* (©1919 by Emmett J. Scott) and *The Unknown Soldiers: Black American Troops in World War I* by Arthur E. Barbeau and Florette Henri (Temple University Press: ©1974 by Temple University).

"THE PASSAGE": Based on the diary and reminiscences of Orval Peyton, who welcomed me into his Tucson, Arizona, home one sunny afternoon in 1987.

"THE CASTLE WALK": In 1913 James Europe and his Society Orchestra were engaged by the celebrated dance team Vernon and Irene Castle, whose brand of ballroom dancing was the rage among New York City's wealthy elite. The Castles ran a dance studio, Castle House, as well as the supper club San Souci.

"RIPONT": The epigraph is from *The Unknown Soldiers: Black American Troops in World War I* by Arthur E. Barbeau and Florette Henri.

TWELVE CHAIRS: Most of these pieces—some in slightly different form—can be found carved on the backs of twelve marble chairs in the lobby of the Federal Court House in Sacramento, California as part of an installation by designer Larry Kirkland.

"HATTIE MCDANIEL ARRIVES AT THE COCONUT GROVE": Hattie McDaniel was the first African-American to win an Oscar (Best Actress in a Supporting Role) for her portrayal of Mammy in the 1939 epic *Gone with the Wind*. For more on her life beyond that fateful evening, see Carlton Jackson's *Hattie: The Life of Hattie McDaniel* (Madison Books, Lanham, Md., 1990).

"FROM YOUR VALENTINE": Imprisoned by the Roman emperor Claudius for acting as an intermediary between forbidden lovers, the future saint Valentinus befriended the jailer's daughter and eventually cured her of her blindness. On the eve of his execution he left her a farewell note, signed "From your Valentine."

"RHUMBA": The epigraph is taken from the opening lines of the song "Yo vengo aquí," written by Francisco Repilado (Compay Segundo) in 1922.

ACKNOWLEDGMENTS

The poems in *American Smooth* first appeared—some in slightly different form—in the following publications:

American Poetry Review: "The Castle Walk," "Noble Sissle's Horn," "Ripont," "The Return of Lieutenant James Reese Europe," and "Variation on Reclamation"; *The American Scholar:* "Looking Up from the Page, I Am Reminded of this Mortal Coil"; *Callaloo:* "Desk Dreams" and "Fox Trot Fridays"; *Columbia Magazine:* "Lullaby"; *Georgia Review:* "Against Flight," "Describe Yourself in Three Words or Less," "Rhumba," and "Samba Summer"; *The Gettysburg Review:* "Quick," "Brown," and "Fox"; *International Quarterly:* "Desert Backyard" and "Eliza, Age 10, Harlem"; *Meridian:* "Count to Ten and We'll Be There"; *Mid-American Review:* "Driving Through"; *The New Yorker:* "All Souls'," "American Smooth," and "Hattie McDaniel Arrives at the Coconut Grove"; *Ploughshares:* "Bolero," "Mercy," and "Now"; *Poetry:* "Cozy Apologia," "Evening Primrose," "I Have Been a Stranger in a Strange Land," "Reverie in Open Air," "The Seven Veils of Salomé," and "Soprano"; *The Progressive:* "From Your Valentine"; *River Styx:* "Alfonzo Prepares to Go Over the Top"; *Shenandoah:* "Heart to Heart" and "Meditation at Fifty Yards, Moving Target"; *Slate:* "Blues in Half-Tones, 3/4 Time," "Ta Ta Cha Cha," and "Two for the Montrose Drive-In"; *The Southern Review:* "La Chapelle. 92nd Division. Ted."

"Chocolate," "Eliza, Age 10, Harlem," "Evening Primrose," and "Soprano" appeared in the chapbook *Evening Primrose: Selected Poems,* Tunheim Santrizos Company (Minneapolis, Minnesota), 1998.

"Chocolate" is also part of *Seven for Luck,* a song cycle for soprano and orchestra, lyrics by Rita Dove, music by John Williams, and first appeared in the program of the song cycle's world premiere with the Boston Symphony at Tanglewood, July 25, 1998.

"Sic Itur ad Astra" appeared in the May 7, 1995 issue of *The Washington Post Sunday Magazine,* in conjunction with the cover article by Walt Harrington titled "The Shape of Her Dreaming: Rita Dove Writes a Poem."

All section epigraphs are remarks made by Lieutenant Commander Tuvok of the Federation Starship *Voyager*—a character in the television series *Star Trek: Voyager* (1995–2001).

Grateful acknowledgment is given to the University of Virginia's Shannon Center for Advanced Studies for affording me time to concentrate on poetry, as well as to Kate Webber and Erika Baxter, who found research materials and books that "time had forgot," David Gies for checking my Spanish, and to Tussi and John Kluge for allowing me the haven of their estate in the Scottish Highlands. Last but certainly not least, a hug and a wink to all my ballroom dancing friends.

BIOGRAPHICAL NOTE

Rita Dove, former Poet Laureate of the United States, is the recipient of many honors, among them the Pulitzer Prize, the National Humanities Medal and the Heinz Award. Among her recent publications are the poetry collection *On the Bus with Rosa Parks* and the drama *The Darker Face of the Earth*. She is Commonwealth Professor of English at the University of Virginia.

Additional biographical information is available on the Web at www.people.virginia.edu/~rfd4b/.